No More Fear

The Battle to Keep My Sanity

JAZMIN GILMORE

WESTBOW·
PRESS
A DIVISION OF THOMAS NELSON
& ZONDERVAN

Cover image by Worldview Enterprises LLC

Scriptures taken from the Holy Bible, New International Version®,
NIV®. Copyright © 1973, 1978, 1984, 2011 by Biblica, Inc.™
Used by permission of Zondervan. All rights reserved worldwide.
www.zondervan.com The "NIV" and "New International
Version" are trademarks registered in the United States Patent
and Trademark Office by Biblica, Inc.™ All rights reserved.

WestBow Press books may be ordered through booksellers or by contacting:

WestBow Press
A Division of Thomas Nelson & Zondervan
1663 Liberty Drive
Bloomington, IN 47403
www.westbowpress.com
1 (866) 928-1240

ISBN: 978-1-4908-4464-0 (sc)
ISBN: 978-1-4908-4465-7 (e)

Library of Congress Control Number: 2014912598

Printed in the United States of America.

WestBow Press rev. date: 07/23/2014

Contents

Dedication

I dedicate this book to God, without whom I would not have made it this far. If it had not been for God, I would have lost my mind and may have been locked up in a mental institution. I thank God for delivering me from that fate.

I thank God for looking past my flaws, thoughts, feelings, and actions. I thank him for looking at my heart and seeing the love I had for him. He gave me the endurance, perseverance, and confidence to not give up but to hope for freedom and know he would never leave me or forsake me.

I thank God for giving me a mind to change everything about me that's not like him and to be more like him so I could serve him in spirit and truth. God is my life!

I love my mother, Jennifer, so much, and I thank God for giving me such a strong, loving, nurturing, truthful mother who helped instill in me the knowledge that with God, I can make it through anything. She believed in me and helped push me to pursue my dreams. I would not trade her for the world.

I am so blessed to have my dad Stevie and stepdad Ronnie in my life. I thank God for them being there to encourage me to press forward to a bright future and not give up or let anything hold me down.

I thank my siblings—Gabrielle, Ashley, and Leonard—and Leonard's wife, Keiera, and my church family, Breath of Life Ministry. Thank you for the encouragement you provided along the way. I love you all.

I thank my nieces and nephews; I want them to know they should always put God first and never let the Enemy, people, or even themselves hold them back from accomplishing their dreams.

Meeshell, I thank you so much for your time and dedication to help edit my book.

Introduction

In this world, the word *afraid* has taken on a whole new meaning. What is the difference between being afraid and being fearful? You can be afraid of many things, including snakes, heights, insects, clowns, unemployment, losing a loved one, losing your home, and so on, but being afraid does not take control of your character or spirit. Fear, however, is a spirit sent by the Devil to control your character and your way of thinking and to make you unable to function in society. Fear can sabotage you emotionally, physically, mentally, and spiritually and immobilize your sense of well-being. Fear definitely knows how to take you by surprise to the point that you don't know how to deal with the fearful phases of your life.

Some people look to drugs to numb the agonizing moments that taunt their minds. Others see psychiatrists in an attempt to hopefully talk their spirit of fear away. Some can't handle the fear they deal with, so they are forced into mental hospitals, where they are sedated and become lifeless souls. Those who feed this spirit of fear may lose touch with reality.

I introduce you to a young woman who grew up in church; her mother is a pastor at a church in Morristown, Tennessee, and she has a stepdad by her side. She has a brother and two sisters. Like her siblings, she was a typical pastor's child who was surrounded by a life of Christianity, though her mother never forced her to live a Christian life.

That young woman is me, Jazmin Gilmore. I was a well-brought-up child. I enjoyed my teen years hanging out with friends and not having a care in the world. Though I was not forced to serve God, I always had this passion for him. As a result, I made up in my mind when I turned eighteen to get closer to God and form a deeper relationship with him. I balanced my Christian walk while in school, and I achieved the biggest thing in the world, finishing high school and setting my sights on college and a career in teaching.

Life, however, threw me an unexpected loop that changed my life in the blink of an eye. What lasted for two months seemed as though it lasted a lifetime as I rode the tormenting roller-coaster of fear.

1

Night Home

It was a beautiful night. Stars illuminated the skies, and I was taking my best friend home from church as usual. In my stepdad's black Yukon, I drove down Jay Byrd Road, a street covered with darkness. I turned onto the dirt road that led to my best friend's trailer home.

As I entered her yard, I heard excitement coming from her living room. Her father and soon-to-be stepmother were drinking and partying. It was ordinary for them to party, so of course I didn't think anything of it. I turned my car around with one thing on my mind—home.

As I drove down Jay Byrd Road toward the highway, my mind was consumed with thoughts of what a great day I had had. Minutes later, I was about four miles from home. All I could think about was resting after the long day. When I was about a mile and a half from home, something suddenly came over me that I had never experienced before. I could hardly breathe, and I felt extremely dizzy. I panicked. A random thought struck me out of nowhere—I believed my car was going to blow up. All of a sudden, the stench of gasoline in my father's car awakened my sense of smell.

I prayed and asked God to please let me make it home, but my panic was unbearable. I had the thought that I should pull over and get out of the car. I immediately pulled onto the shoulder of the pitch-dark highway; cars barely missed mine as they passed. The only thing that was on my mind was escape. I struggled to take off my seat belt. When I finally got it off, I hit the unlock button, but for some reason, the door wouldn't open. A mixture of anxiety and adrenaline overwhelmed me. I decided to crawl out the window. I hit the gritty pavement head first. I got up and began to run away from the car.

I was in pure darkness. A car or two passed but didn't stop. I was terrified. I had to decide to run a mile and a half to home or stay there. I fiddled around in my pocket for my phone and found it to my relief. I dialed my stepfather's number, but he didn't pick up. Panic set in again. I called my stepdad again. Still no answer. I called my sister, but she didn't answer either. I wondered, *What do I do?* Tears rolled down my face, and I was overwhelmed by the thought of dying.

At that moment, I began to talk to God, and all of a sudden, I heard a sound coming from my phone; it was my stepdad. I immediately answered and told him what had happened and where I was. He didn't waste any time; he was there in less than five minutes with my little sister. I got in my sister's car, and my stepdad got in the Yukon and drove it back to the house.

After I got home, the panic, the dizziness, and the anxiety left as quickly as they had come. I called my mother, who was also my pastor, because she was out of town taking care of my brother. I told her what had happened, and she encouraged me and let me know God would always protect me.

When I got off the phone, I asked my stepdad repeatedly to take me to the hospital. He refused. He said, "Jazmin, there's nothing wrong with you. If I took you there, they'd lock you up in a crazy house." I asked my stepdad if he had checked the car, and he told me there was no gas leakage. The car didn't smell like gas either. I couldn't believe it. I began to replay those terrifying moments of being in that car, and then my eyes opened. It was impossible for me to have smelled gas because I have a disorder called anosmia, the loss of the sense of smell.

I thought back to when I was trying to open the car door; I realized the reason why the door hadn't opened was because I had pulled the lever and pulled the door toward me instead of pulling the lever and pushing the door away from me. But it all had seemed so real—the smell, the feeling—but I soon realized it was just an illusion.

That night, fear had come up the doorsteps to my thoughts, and fear wanted to take up residence in the rooms of my mind. It was then that I realized my journey with fear was just beginning.

2

Dap

My mother and stepdad had picked up my friend, my sister, and me from school. They laughed and chatted as we rode home. My stepdad had the radio on his favorite station, and all was well. I was surrounded by people I loved and who loved me, but I felt a void inside.

I tried to engage in conversation, but it was as if I could participate in it only so far, until I was back in my own world. I looked around my stepdad's Yukon and saw the faces of my family and friend. It didn't seem real. I wanted so badly to smile, to engage in conversation, and enjoy it. I wanted so badly to feel whole, but I was trapped like a treasure concealed in a boxed wrapped in an enigma of chains with a padlock holding it tight with no key to open it.

I slouched in my seat, looking up at nothing. I felt so lethargic. All I wanted to do was sleep, but that required me to be by myself, and I wasn't going to have that. I felt I needed to stay as close to my mom as possible.

In twenty minutes, DAP was going to start. DAP stood for Deliverance and Peace; it was a meeting at my church anyone could attend to share feelings, eat, and fellowship. No matter how sleepy I was, I made up my mind to go to that meeting.

As we approached the stop sign leading to my house, my mom turned to me, stared, and asked, "Jazmin, what's wrong with you? You don't look like yourself. You need to get some sleep."

As soon as she said that, my heart began to race and anxiety began to take its toll. I knew what she was saying was right, but I said, "Nothing's wrong, Mom. I'm going with y'all to DAP, so I can't sleep and miss out on that."

"No, you're staying home," was her response.

We pulled up by the garage. My stepdad was dropping me and my sixteen-year-old sister off. I begged, "Mom, please let me go! Don't leave me!"

"No, Jazmin, you're staying here, and that's it!"

I got out of the car and backed up so they could pull away and head to DAP. As I saw them disappear down the road, tears gushed down my face. I quickly got in the house and sat on the couch. I tried to rest my body, but I couldn't. I rocked myself back and forth; my stomach felt like it had a million butterflies in it. I couldn't sit still. I moved from one chair to another. I tried to close my eyes to sleep, but it was as if sleep didn't exist for me anymore.

My sister came down the stairs, sat on the couch across from me, and turned on the TV. I tried to act as though I were fine. She didn't say anything to me, but her look said everything. I couldn't stay still any longer. My chest began to hurt, and my stomach became queasy. I grabbed my phone, went to my mother's room, and sat on the edge of her bed. I called her and my stepdad, but they didn't pick up. I wanted to tell them that my chest was hurting and that I didn't know what was wrong with me.

I put my phone down and lay on my side. My thoughts were racing a thousand miles an hour, which caused even more anxiety. I felt I couldn't breathe. My chest began to throb even more, and my right side became numb. The side of my face was drooping gradually. It was as if I couldn't talk. Thoughts of dying right there on my mother's bed tortured me. *What do I do?* I asked myself. Something told me to pray. I began losing the feeling on my right side. I worked up the strength to sit up, pray, quote Scriptures, and rebuke the Enemy.

Why am I going through this? I wondered. *I don't want to be like this anymore! How can I turn these emotions off?* I refused to stop trusting in God regardless of my inability to fathom why I was experiencing such tremendous fear.

Next, I was moving around while praying. The nervousness and chest pains along with the queasiness began to subside. I headed back to the living room and asked Gabby, "Can I watch something on TV?" My sister was devoted to Disney Channel, however, surprisingly, she said yes and went upstairs. I grabbed the remote and turned to TBN. I was at war with the Enemy, and all I could think of was hearing the Word of God and praising him to gain some strength. I realized that if I had stayed in bed and not prayed, who knows, I could have been admitted to a hospital or maybe even lost my life. Christ saved me that night.

3

Kids' Bible Study

It was Bible study time; I was supposed to teach about ten kids one night, but I didn't feel up to the challenge. The kids tugged on me left and right. My body was so drained because of the toll anxiousness had taken on me. I was trying to maintain the perky Jazmin the kids normally saw, but I failed at that. The children wondered what the night's lesson was going to be. Unfortunately, I had been robbed of the opportunity to prepare a lesson that day due to horrid thoughts of having a heart attack, stroke, or even dying. I had to think quickly of a lesson to teach the kids, and one came to me—Gideon's army. The kids' enthusiasm sunk, however; they realized Miss Jazmin wasn't acting normally. Sarah raised her hand. "Miss Jazmin? are you okay?"

"Of course," I said. "Miss Jazmin is just tired." But I knew I was beyond tired. I was listless, hoping for the night to end. It wasn't even ten minutes into class that I realized I wasn't going to do it. I told the kids they could have a free day, and they jumped around with excitement. All they knew was that Miss Jazmin was the best teacher, but I desperately needed rescuing from the dreary cloud that hovered over me.

I lay down on the floor while the kids jumped, played, and laughed all around me. "Get up, Miss Jazmin! Let's play a game!" said Trinity as she tugged on me.

There was no way I could. "Not right now." They couldn't see the agony that tortured me; all they knew was that I wasn't acting like myself. I looked around with envy at the children, wishing I could be a kid again with no worries, just living life to the fullest. But I knew that was impossible.

4

One Particular Sunday

One Sunday, I woke up to a throbbing in my body. I had slept restlessly; I had tossed and turned the whole night. Not a single godly thought was running through my mind that morning; it was filled with all sorts of rebelliousness toward God. My thoughts were telling me I didn't need to go to church. *What for?* I thought. *God isn't real. I should just stay home because he's not going to protect me.*

"Jazmin!" my mom yelled from downstairs. "Wake up! It's time to get dressed for Sunday service." I had to get dressed and be on my way to church. I got to Breath of Life ministries, where my mom is the pastor over the faithful and devoted. I dreaded going in; I knew people would swarm over me, the pastors' daughter, and give me greetings, hugs, and kisses and try to engage me in conversation.

On that particular Sunday, I couldn't have cared less about showing love; all I wanted was just to be home. I took a seat in the back pew even though I normally sat in front. I looked around and watched people come in. Some were smiling and anticipating what the day was going to bring, while others had nonchalant expressions that clearly said, *I'm just here to be here.*

I could really tell those who were expecting God to do something amazing in their lives that Sunday morning. Deep down, I had that expectation, that hope, for change to take place in my life, but my mind was clouded with thoughts of whether God would do it for me and even if he was real. Some were hugging each other and talking about the week before, and others were making plans for the future. A number of people came up to me with hugs and kisses.

Church was going to start in a matter of minutes. People claimed their seats and waited for the service to begin. The pianist motioned for the praise team to grace the stage with their presence. She looked at me first, as I was the head praise team leader. With all the thoughts going through my mind, I didn't want to be up there, but I knew the service must go on. I stepped onto the stage to sing to God when my mind was bombarded with cusswords. I felt God was going to strike me down any minute. I thought repeatedly, *God, please forgive me*, but that didn't stop the words from coming. I timidly grabbed the microphone when I heard the melody of the first song. People were staring at the praise team, waiting for God's presence in our voices to usher them in the Spirit. It was time to sing. It took every nerve in my body to work up enough courage to sing to my God after I felt I'd disrespected him in every way imaginable. I didn't feel worthy. I felt that I was the biggest sinner in church, but I had to act as if nothing were wrong. I looked at the people lifting their hands and singing to God, dancing unto him, and rejoicing. Tears rolled down their faces as they enjoyed the presence of God and feeling their cares lifting off them. I became so envious. *Why can't I experience that freedom? Why can't my cares be taken away?*

The song ended. It was time for the praise team to sit. My mother got up and preached, but I wasn't paying attention to one word she was saying. I was ready to leave.

The next part of the service was communion; everyone in the congregation received a cracker and a mini cup of grape juice. The grape juice represented Jesus' blood, while the cracker represented his body. Communion is symbolic of Christ's death and resurrection. We took communion very seriously; we all knew that in order to receive communion, we had to be in right standing with God. I knew I wasn't going to receive communion. Before my mother read the Scriptures and consumed the juice and cracker, they sang a song.

> I know it was the blood
> That saved me
> One day when I was lost
> He died up on that cross
> I know it was the blood for me

I was sitting and listening to the words, and as I was thinking, I went back and forth in my mind with the Enemy.

ENEMY: You know it wasn't Christ's blood that saved you.

ME: I'm not going to listen to you! I know it was Christ's blood.

ENEMY: God didn't die on the cross, especially not for you.

ME: Yes, Christ died on the cross for my sins.

ENEMY: He's not even real! Just go ahead and curse God.

ME: God is real!

ENEMY: Curse God!

Uncontrollably, cusswords toward God surfaced in my mind. I quickly asked God to forgive me, but those cusswords kept on surfacing in my mind. I was so overwhelmed at that moment that it felt as though my mind were on fire. Tears filled my eyes. I tried to hold them back, but it was impossible. I darted to the bathroom before anyone realized I was crying. I stood in the corner with my back against the wall. I felt that everything was caving in on me. I felt weak as emotions tugged me from every direction. I wondered when this would be over.

5

Classroom

What should I do? Should I leave or should I stay home? It was only thirty minutes until my class started. I had had no energy to get out of bed, but I knew I better make myself go to class. I couldn't risk losing my financial aid due to a lack of attendances. I used all my strength to get out of bed. My feet hit the floor like two boulders. I felt giant weights pressing down on every ounce of my body. I finally worked up the strength to make my way to the bathroom. I gazed in the mirror and quickly looked away in disgust. I looked like a dead soul. I could hardly look in the mirror without feeling like throwing up. I quickly brushed my hair into a simple ponytail. I'd become accustomed to that style since it didn't require much thought. My mind was bombarded with thoughts of worthlessness anyway.

I threw on some clothes and walked anxiously out my front door to my car. Looking over my shoulder, I made sure no one was trying to approach me. After reaching school, I headed to the classroom and looked at the clock. I was ten minutes late, but I didn't care. I entered the classroom just as the teacher was starting to lecture. The students turned their heads as I walked by them. My classmates looked at me as if they had never seen me before. I felt like an exchange student from a foreign place, but I tried my best to ignore the expressions on their faces.

I settled in at my desk, grabbed my pencil and paper, and thanked God I had my Bible, which I pulled out of my bag. I breathed deeply as I mentally repeated the Scripture, "God didn't give me the spirit of fear but of power, love, and a sound mind." For the first time in a long time, I was in control of my thoughts, and I was relieved.

I took deep breaths and began to relax. Ten more minutes passed; my teacher was lecturing on how to operate Microsoft Word. All of a sudden, nervousness took over my body. The next thing I knew, my teacher's words were a foreign language. I didn't understand him at all. The only thing I heard were loud words, *Get out! There's a bomb!* I look around frantically. I didn't understand why everyone else was so calm. *Didn't they hear what I just heard?* I didn't want to make a lot of commotion while class was going on, so I tried to get a grip on my emotions. Then I heard it again: *Get out now! Hurry! Move now!* I wondered if I should leave or stay. My mother's words quickly came back to me: "Face it. What you're fighting is a demon!" I grabbed my Bible and opened it. I knew people had to be looking at me as if I were crazy, but that didn't matter; I was battling something within. I was desperately trying to find a Scripture to fight off those thoughts, but the words *Get out!* became even more vehement.

I was trying to restrain myself from following my mind's command, but thoughts of leaving became more intense. I wasn't able to find one Scripture to reign over my mind. *Get out!* rang in my ears so loudly that I couldn't take it. My desire to fight my thoughts went out the window. I grabbed my things and started briskly out the door. My thoughts grew arms and legs and catapulted me through the classroom door. My stomach knotted, my knees buckled, and tears began rolling down my face.

The cold weather outside school chilled me. I felt like falling down, curling up in a ball, and acting as if I didn't exist. The word *suicide* taunted my mind. I remember thinking, *The Devil is a lie that's never an option* as my tears drenched my clothes and my nose ran uncontrollably. I didn't understand. I remember repeating, "Why me?"

I called my mom; I told her class had been dismissed early and I was leaving. I lied to her because I didn't want her to know I had once again given in to that spirit of fear.

6

Can't Go to Sleep

One particular night, I was lying in bed trying to fall asleep. I was tossing and turning; the Enemy within was having a field day. I couldn't shake the feeling of being rejected by God. Cusswords welled up in my mind; I cursed God but immediately apologized for that. It was a tug of war; one minute, I was cursing God, but the next minute, I was praying for forgiveness because deep inside, I knew I didn't mean what I was thinking.

I couldn't take it. I hopped out of bed and headed downstairs to my parents' room at one in the morning. There I was, all of eighteen, and I was climbing into bed with my mom. I felt like a five-year-old seeking protection from a big bad monster. I didn't want to tell her what was going on in my mind again, so I kept it to myself; I told her I just couldn't sleep.

I was there less than five minutes; I couldn't lie still. I headed back to my room. I knew not even my mother or stepfather could protect me from the Enemy within. Back in my bed, I stared into space and managed to drift off to sleep.

The next morning, I awoke exhausted, weak, and defeated. My mother wanted me to go with her that morning to the bank. I didn't feel like it, but my mom insisted. When we got back, I couldn't take it. I sat in the living room feeling that I was going to throw up. My mom fixed me a bowl of chili, but the thought of food left an undesirable taste in my mouth. I asked my mom to sit on the couch, I grasped her legs and told her what was wrong with me, that I felt I had been rejected by God and was not worthy. I felt embarrassed telling her, but something urged me to release my feelings.

"Jazmin, you're not rejected by God," she said. "God loves you. The Enemy plays on your fears, and he knows you fear hurting God and getting rejected by him, so he will use that to get to you."

The God who lived in my mother began speaking loud and clear. The words he spoke through my mother touched my soul. At that moment, I was set free from any thoughts of rejection.

7

Doctor's Visit

"Jazmin," my mother told me, "there's nothing wrong with you; you're not fighting something physical but something spiritual. To prove this, I'll take you to the doctor." Her words rang in my mind as I fought the pain in my chest and the knots in my stomach. Always feeling nervous had become normal for me, so finding out the reason for it would be a great relief.

As my mother drove me to Health Star Medical, I thought, *Jazmin, are you ready for the news you might get?* I didn't want them to find anything wrong with me physically, but if they didn't, that would mean I was mentally disturbed, one label I refused to accept. My mind and my body were at stake, and one way or another, no matter what they told me was wrong or not wrong, I just wanted a key to unlock the doors of fear that held my mind, soul, and body captive.

I quickly signed in and sat in the crowded waiting room to wait for my name to be called. The faces of the other patients began to fade, as if I were suddenly all alone in the room. Even what my mother was saying to me faded into the back of my mind. All I could hear was the anxiousness screaming out my name in a never-ending taunt that made me want to gag.

I was in my own world; anxiety began to feed on my mind. I asked myself "what if" questions—*What if they find this or that? What if I have to go on pills?* Such questions consumed every bit of my brain, leaving no room for positive thoughts.

I came back to reality when the nurse called my name. My mother and I entered a room full of cotton swabs, tongue depressors, ear thermometers, and latex gloves; it was adorned with posters that offered information about health. My mother and I sat. A nurse came in to write down why I had come in, but I knew she wouldn't understand. She left the room. My mother and I waiting for the doctor to come in. I was trying to stay calm and relaxed, which was difficult.

My mom and I were deep in conversation about life when we were interrupted by a knock. The doctor came in, and I shared with her the difficult things I had been dealing with, including dizziness, weakness, chest pain, and other symptoms. She analyzed me and tested me before she left us in the room. The doctor who carried my diagnosis in the palm of her hand came back shortly. My heart was beating as if it were going to jump out of my shirt any minute.

"Well, Jazmin, do you counsel?" asked the doctor. We talked for a while about things that didn't seem relevant to what I was experiencing. Finally, she looked at me as if she were confused. "Jazmin, there's nothing wrong with you. You're perfectly fine. But if you don't grab hold of yourself, the counselor is going to need a psychiatrist." Her words hit me like a freight train; if I didn't shake this off, I was going to need a psychiatrist. She was very blunt. I looked at my mother. Her look told me silently, *Jazmin, you're dealing with something beyond reality, something demonic.*

That day, I grabbed hold of what my doctor and my mother told me. I realized that it was time for me to put my faith into action. It was time to trust that God would guide me and help me become free, especially from the spirit of fear that was attempting to destroy my life.

8

Trip to the Health Store

My anxiety became unbearable. My never-ending nervousness was attacking my body. I always felt queasy. I had no appetite, and I often felt I couldn't breathe. I thought I couldn't take it any longer. I hoped there was something I could take to free me from these feelings at least for a second.

I went to the health store, thinking that surely they would have something I could use. I thought that peace would be mine once I held an antidote for anxiety in my hand. I scanned the shelves as I waited to talk to a clerk. *What do I need to take?* I thought I could simply buy a quick fix.

Five minutes later, an employee came up to me. "How may I help you?" I told her about my symptoms, and she knew just what to give me. "You need magnesium pills to take care of your stress and anxiety." At that point, anything sounded good, so I said, "Why not?" I bought them with high expectations that I finally had something that would rid me of my symptoms. I opened the bottle, shook out one pill, and took it. As time went by, I couldn't sense any difference in me, so I thought, *Why not take two more?*

I took the pills for three days. It felt that they were trying to work, but I thought I had wasted my money. I needed something stronger. I kept getting the feeling that I shouldn't depend on pills. I had to seek counseling for this, so I sought out my mother. I didn't know how to approach her; I was afraid of what she might say. I didn't know if I was ready to hear the truth. I eased my way toward her, working up the nerve to express my concerns. "Mom, do you think I should take a magnesium pill today?" She looked at me and sighed. "I've been taking them for about a week now," I said, "and I kind of feel a difference."

My mother paused. "Well, honey, you can do what you feel like." I was shocked. Did my mom say what I wanted to hear, that it was okay for me to take those pills? I was going to take those words and run. I said "Okay" and headed out of the room, but before I could close the door, she said, "Jazmin, even if those pills seem to be working, it's only going to be temporary."

That's my mom, I thought.

"It's going to be temporary. It will get worse, and then you'll have to find a stronger pill and then an even stronger pill. You'll be chasing peace you'll never be able to reach through pills. You choose. It's up to you to face your fear and not look for a substitute for God. Or you can do it your way and continue to run from this never-ending fear that will soon overpower you."

My mother always gave me the raw truth; she never cut corners. You could either apply the truth and save your life or not apply it and lose your life. It didn't take much for me that day. I made up my mind to stop taking those magnesium pills. *Let the games begin*, I thought as I geared up to battle my opponent, fear.

9

Hairdresser

I regularly went to my hairdresser to get my usual relaxer and flat-iron treatment. I sat in the chair while the hairdresser combed my hair and talked about school and God. But one particular visit was different from all others. I drove to the New Style Hair Salon, put my car in park, took a deep breath, and chanted to myself, *I can do this. I can do this. God, you are with me. I will not let fear take up residence in my life.* I stepped out of my car though my mind and body were telling me to get back in and head home. All I wanted to do was crawl under the covers and hide, but at that moment, I was taking a stand. I walked into the salon, took a deep breath, and sat.

Things were going as usual, but I had to fight the urge to leave. I heard a voice in my head. *Leave! A man is going to come and kill you.* That was all I could take. I got up and headed for the door, not even saying good-bye. I went to my car. As I got in, I stopped and began talking to myself. *Jazmin, you don't want to give into this and be defeated.* I called my mother. Thank God she answered. I told her what I was experiencing. She told me not to give in. "The minute you give in, the fear gets power over you, and then you become its slave. Instead, stand face to face with it and don't back down."

I took her words to heart; I refused to allow fear to overcome me. I returned to the salon. It was time for me to get in the chair and for the beautician to put my hair relaxer in. From then on, I decided I didn't want to be a victim of fear. I stayed until she finished. That day, I realized that I was a conqueror and that I would not give in to fear.

10

Praise Team Rehearsal

I drove my 1997 green Ford Explorer to pick up my best friend, Jo. She and I wanted some prayer time before praise team rehearsal, which started in an hour and a half. I needed this prayer time more than anything, but I was amazed that she wanted to join me since I hadn't been acting myself lately. I'd been in distress, pondering if I was going to live to see another night.

My right arm had been giving me problems all day; the pain would ease up in my arm, but it would radiate thru my chest. Once again, however, I didn't say a thing about it. Jo sat quietly in the passenger seat. We were silent as we drove. Suddenly, she looked at me. "Jazmin, what's wrong with you? If you continue to be all dreary like this, I'm not going to hang out with you anymore."

Her words penetrated my heart; I couldn't believe what she had just said. I was speechless. I realized she was right; who would want to be around someone who was anxious, fearful, dreary, and depressed? Still, that didn't stop me from looking at her with disgust. I yelled, "Do you really think I want to be like this? If I could turn these emotions off, I would have weeks ago! I didn't choose to be like this!" Tears streamed down my face. I felt all alone; I thought no one understood me.

She was shocked. "I'm sorry, Jazmin. I didn't mean to say it." She put her arms around me as we were stopped at a red light.

We pulled up to the Breath of Life Ministry. Its doors seemed to stare me down. I walked into the sanctuary. I planned on using every minute of our prayer time in spite of how I felt and the thoughts racing through my mind. My arms stretched wide as I again worshipped and praised God. That took everything out of me, but I didn't let it stop me. I suddenly felt a calmness in my whole body and an unexplained chill. Once again, I knew I was in the presence of God.

The doors of the sanctuary sprang open; the praise team was coming in to practice. I didn't even realize I had been down on my knees praying for an hour. Tonia, the organist, announced, "Time for practice." Everyone headed to the stage; I managed to hold in the emotions I had felt caused by God's presence while we practiced. We hugged and said hello to each other. The first song was, "You Are Great." Tonia played the organ, and I led the song. As the words came from my mouth, I felt the Spirit of God stirring inside me. The chills came back. Next thing I knew, I was singing with more passion than ever. I forgot where I was; I was in my own personal worship service.

I looked around and saw how the glory of God was touching not only me but was also having a domino effect. Miss Linda's eyes were filled with tears as she waved her hands. Carter had her eyes closed as she reverenced God. Jo was moving back and forth, and Tonia was playing as she had never played before. God's presence was so overwhelming that I couldn't stay in one place. I took off running uncontrollably around the church as I sang into the microphone.

Hours went by before we finally quieted down and enjoyed the peace God had left us with. Every thought and pain that I had brought into church had gone. I was in heaven.

Practice was over. As we all headed for the door, Miss Linda said, "Thank you for letting God use you." I thanked God for allowing me to feel his presence and achieve a breakthrough. I knew I was getting closer to my complete deliverance.

11

Bomb in the Church

As a church leader, I had a key to the building. At that time in my life, that key became vital to me keeping my sanity. I pulled into the empty church parking lot, anticipating my personal prayer time with God. I knew with no doubt at all that if I could get to the altar and fall prostrate before God with no one there to distract me, everything would be alright.

I unlocked the door, went in, and locked the door behind me. I rushed to turn on the lights in the dark sanctuary. *Okay*, I thought, *time for my breakthrough.* I walked toward the altar and faced the podium with my arms stretched wide. Words of praise and exaltation to God began to flow out of my mouth. I began to dance before him, tears unashamedly running down my cheeks. I began to lose myself. But suddenly, I was shaken by the word *bomb*! I couldn't breathe. I was attacked by an anxiety that shocked me from my toes to my head. *What if this is God telling me to escape?*

I picked up my things and headed for the door. I was trying to unlock the door to save my life, but I couldn't unlock it. Instead, I gripped the doorknob as warning signs went off in my head. Something deeper than my fears was speaking to me. What God had put inside of me told me, *No, don't run. Stay in this church. You're going to be fine. There's no bomb.* When God speaks to us, he doesn't bring about fear that causes anxiety; his Word says he doesn't give us the spirit of fear. I realized the Enemy was trying to get me to think God had warned me about a bomb, but I knew it wasn't. I loosened my grip of the knob and pulled my key out of the lock. I still felt anxiety running through my body, but I headed for the front pew.

My hand started to go numb again, my chest started to throb even more, but I was determined to listen to God and not allow my thoughts to overrule him. My flesh wanted to leave, but my spirit was standing bold in faith; I knew God was my protector. Isaiah 54:17 tells us, "No weapon formed against you shall prosper." I thought that if the church was going to blow up, at least I would go to heaven, and if the church didn't explode, I would know I had conquered another day.

I sat, filled with every emotion, but I prayed. I had faith he would protect me and heal my body, mind, and spirit. I was standing on his Word even though at first it felt that my pains were intensifying and my mind was telling me it wasn't a good decision to stay. Nonetheless, I believed in something I couldn't see, hoping for victory against all odds.

Once again, I began to dance and praise God in spite of my numbness and chest pains. I thanked God even though my thoughts were urging me to leave. In three minutes, my anxiety started subsiding. In seven minutes, my chest pains began to leave. In thirteen minutes, the feeling in my arms came back, and after fifteen minutes, I was completely free of negative thoughts and pain.

When I exited the church, it wasn't because of fear or anxiety or pain; it was because I was no longer being stalked by thoughts of something that was trying to kill me. I walked out that door fearless, bold, at peace, and most definitely victorious. It was all because God was right by my side.

12

Church Van

The day had been rough. I had fought the demons and thoughts of suicide plaguing my mind. I battled all day to free myself of these foul thoughts that had me cursing God for no reason.

I was anticipating a church function in Knoxville; I was determined to have time to enjoy God and hopefully forget everything that tormented me. I wanted to focus on God.

That evening, the Breath of Life met in front of our church to get in the van to go to Knoxville. My mother was going to be speaking that night. We were packed in the van like sardines. My best friend and I sat in the back, talking about our days and chatting about old times. Conversation like that was just what I needed to get my mind off my worries.

After my friend and I stopped talking, however, I was again stuck in my own world, fighting to stay positive. I looked out the window and admired the beautiful trees we were passing. I heard a voice. *God is not real! You might as well give up! He never was real! You have been serving God for nothing!* Those thoughts overtook me to the point that I felt I'd lost my identity as a Christian. Though serving God has always been my chosen path, those awful thoughts weighed heavily on my heart.

My eyes began to water. I decided I couldn't let these thoughts override the God inside me who had deposited something in me. I knew he was real; I refused to allow the Enemy to convince me otherwise. I knew I was at war. Every dart the Enemy threw at me went back full throttle at him. I fought with my only weapon, the Word of God. It took me just a second to remember the passage in the Bible in which Satan tried to get Jesus to sin in every way, but because Jesus knew the Word of God and was the Word, he quoted Scripture to Satan, having faith in what he said. Satan couldn't do anything but flee.

Mine was a war with no doubt that I was going to win with faith. My chest throbbed as my inner battle raged. I was quickly able to conquer my fears, and my faith in God was restored.

I made sure no one around me noticed my inner torment, but I couldn't hold back my joyous tears. I, Jazmin Gilmore, had put the Word of God in action; I had been victorious against the Enemy. I turned and wiped my tears so no one would notice. My best friend looked at me. She was concerned but yet comforting as she told me that God had just told her about my battles with doubt and that he was proud of me.

I was overwhelmed with emotions; I began crying again. I knew God had spoken to her. As I hugged her, I realized that God had given me confirmation that he was real, and my spirits were uplifted for the rest of the ride.

We reached our destination. I got out the van with the others to get ready for the service, but I couldn't shake an unbearable pain that had penetrated me. I thought, *God, you are the healer, and I'm expecting you to deliver me from those feelings.*

The service started with the usual Scripture readings and prayer followed by praise and worship. I thought this was an opportunity to lose myself in God. They were singing a fast song, and I began to clap my hands, open my mouth, and stomp my feet to bless the Lord. But it seemed that the more I praised, the worse my pain became. In spite of the pain, however, I let God take control. I was soon in a place with God no one could take me out of. I lost total control of my hands and feet. I felt like Joshua must have felt when he marched around the walls of Jericho. The walls of my infirm spirit and anxiety were going to fall. I thanked God while I danced before him, and his presence fell upon me like never before.

The chest pains that had been harassing me all day and night ceased, and I was consumed with joy. God had accomplished that; he had answered my prayer. That night, through expectation and praise, my chains of infirmity broke. From that day on, I haven't had chest pains since this day. Once God delivers you, you don't go back.

13

Between the Events

Even as an eighteen-year-old, I held many positions in my church. I was a praise dance choreographer, Sunday school teacher, kids' Bible study teacher, and praise team leader while attending college full time. I kept up this level of activity in spite of having to battle my fears. I often asked God why I was going through this fearful phase in my life.

Psychologists say that people often experience dreaded fear due to tragic circumstances they have experienced. Rape, sexual abuse, other crimes, and the death of loved ones can deprive people of their sense of security and peace of mind. However, I had never suffered such tragedies; the people in my life had always treated me with respect. I had a great life, a loving family, and a sense of security. I loved my life.

When fear invaded my space without a warrant, I realized that fear doesn't care; its goal is to ravage its victims in every way possible. At times, I felt all alone even though I was surrounded by family and friends. I often felt I was all by myself in a box closed off from the world. I felt pain, anxiety, and fear of the unknown that seemed to overtake me day by day. I was distraught emotionally and lacked a sense of self-worth. I would go days without eating because the thought of food made me want to throw up. I lost an extreme amount of weight and began looking like a totally different person.

It got so bad that I didn't care what I looked like. I always loved doing my hair and dressing up, but during this period of fear, I couldn't have cared less how I looked. I always felt totally drained. Fear took the life right out of me. Every day was a struggle; I looked to sleep to soothe me, but at times, even that didn't work. I cried all the time because I didn't know how to deal with my feelings. I asked God, "What's going on with me? I know you didn't bring me this far to leave me." However, at times I didn't get an answer back from God.

I can definitely say, however, that I wouldn't have overcome my feelings without God's help and the help of essential people in my life, including my mother and my best friend. I have learned through this journey of fear to not "feed" my feelings, emotions, or thoughts. For instance, you feed a newborn baby so it will grow up strong and healthy, but I was determined not to feed fear, so it can grow and consume my life. I had to face those things that taunted me. That wasn't easy, and some days I did give into the fear and stayed home. However, I knew I had to continue to push day by day and do the opposite of what my negative thoughts wanted me to do.

I am now twenty-two. I have been free of that spirit of fear going on four years. I look back and thank God for the experience, which got me to a place where I am now steadfast in the faith. It enhanced my relationship with God and molded me into a powerful woman of God who knows who she is in Christ. It was worth the anxiety, pain, numbness, and feelings of worthlessness, depression, and loss of control. It was through those feelings, those experiences, that I learned the Devil doesn't care who you are, what you have, and what you know.

My battles with negative thoughts taught me to get on my knees, cry, and pray before God. I learned to hold to what I believe in—God and my deliverance. God said I could obtain freedom if I trusted in him no matter what my life looked like. Now, when the Enemy tries to throw fear at me in any way, I am not fazed because I know who I am and what I possess—the power of the Holy Spirit. I fight him with the Word of God and conquer him.

I didn't overcome fear by taking drugs or seeing a psychiatrist. I didn't overcome fear by giving into it or by running from it. I overcame fear through Christ, who continually strengthens me. I learned how to put his Word into action and experience true deliverance. Once I stopped looking for temporary fixes, I found an everlasting antidote, Jesus Christ.

I look back at those times and can't believe I actually went through them because now I feel so free. I can walk in a store and not have to look over my shoulder to see who's pursuing me. I don't have thoughts that ravage my mind and tell me to leave due to an imaginary threat. I can be alone and at peace in my car or my home with no worries of evil attacking me because I know God is protecting me. I no longer look in the mirror with disgust or feelings of worthlessness because I know I look good and am confident that I am everything God made me to be, his special treasure. I no longer dread getting out of bed, dressing, and doing my hair because I look forward to waking up, browsing through my closet for something interesting to wear, and finding unique styles for my hair. I no longer feel that I can't breathe. I enjoy my night rides home, soaking in the quiet. I took a stand and said, "No more Fear!" I was determined to conquer in my battle and keep my sanity, and I have succeeded.

14

Why Me?

We will always wonder why we go through certain things in life, including sicknesses that will ultimately lead to our deaths. We will wonder why our marriages fail and why we lose jobs. We will wonder why our loved ones, especially children, die. We all are filled with thoughts of "Why me?"

The minute we feel that we're not in control of a situation or crisis, fear can creep through our doors. We blame God for these unexpected crises, slaps in our face. We ask, "Why, God? If you are a loving God, why did you let this happen?" We may say, "If I had never given my life to God, this would not have taken place. Where is God when I need him most?" We may even become angry with God and curse him, blaming him for what we are going through.

We must realize that it's not that God isn't there or doesn't see what we're going through. We must understand that we live in a world full of suffering; we will go through hard times, some of us more than others, whether we give our lives to God or not. It's all because we have sin in this world. It brings forth sickness, disease, and chaos. No matter what we face in our life, we must remember that God sent his only son, Jesus Christ, to die on the tree so we would have the opportunity to live life more abundantly.

No matter what we combat in life—sickness, loss, death, turmoil, pain—God has made sure that as long as we have faith in Christ and have given our lives to him and trust him, we will overcome. In 1 Peter 3:17 kjv, we read, "For it is better, if the will of God be so, that ye suffer for well doing than for evil doing." God revealed to me through that Scripture that we will suffer trials and tribulations, that we will go through very unpleasant things. I asked myself about what Peter said in this Scripture, *Would I rather suffer for good, or would I rather suffer for evil?* To suffer for evil is to be out of the will of God. To be out the will of God means you have not received salvation or you don't have a relationship with God or faith or trust in him. A relationship with God requires you to read the Bible so you can learn and apply the Word to your life, to have a prayer life, fast, and go to church. If you are not fulfilling these obligations, you will suffer for evil, which will eventually lead to death and burning for eternity in hell because of your choice to deny Christ and serve the Enemy. To suffer for good is to be in the will of Christ and have a personal relationship that will increase your faith in him and make you loyal to God by following the truth of his Word.

God gave everyone a choice to suffer for good or evil, so everyone must take personal inventory of himself or herself to determine whether he or she is suffering for good or evil. I chose to suffer for the good because I realize as long as I suffer for Christ and am steadfast in my faith, no matter what challenges I face—sickness, family issues, financial problems, whatever—in the end, I will receive God's blessings.

The apostle Paul said in Romans 8:35 kjv, "Who shall separate us from the love of Christ? Shall tribulation, or distress, or persecution, or fame, or nakedness, or peril, or sword?" This is serious when it comes to your Christian walk. I had to face much distress in my life but stand on the confidence that nothing would separate me from the love of Christ.

Whether I overcome my sufferings on earth or in death, I am assured that as long as I'm suffering for good, I will have the opportunity to make it into the kingdom of heaven. In Revelation 21:4 kjv, we read, "And God will wipe away every tear from their eyes; and there shall be no more death, neither sorrow, nor crying, neither shall there be any more pain: for the former things are passed away." That is something to look forward to, and it will guarantee me a peace that will preserve me through the toughest times.

I have joy that goes beyond any sorrow, but others will experience depression because they're overwhelmed by sorrow. A love surrounds me that will never cease. I will have self-control that will help me make the right decisions. Why would I choose a life to suffer for evil? Why would I go through life with no guarantee that I will make it through my challenges? Why should I look to temporary things to help me through the tough times that will surely fade once the next challenge comes?

Instead of focusing on what you're going through, acknowledge how you got there and take the necessary steps to achieve freedom and peace; that will get you through the tough times before fear finds you.

15

How to Overcome Fear

Here are five steps that will show you how to overcome fear. You may have fear of success, failure, sickness, being alone, or even the unknown, but through my personal experience, I know these steps will work.

1. Realize you can't do it without Christ.
2. Realize who you are and what you possess.
3. Realize that what you're dealing with is a demonic spirit.
4. Transform your thoughts and put your weapons to work.
5. Be steadfast in the faith.

The main questions are: Do you believe? Do you have faith? Are you willing to trust God and cast your cares upon him? Your answers to these simple questions will challenge your faith and trust in God in every area.

It will take your determination and willingness to depend on God to get you through those tough times, and you will. The Enemy will come into your mind to make you feel like the steps you're taking for change have no effect, just as the Enemy did to me. But I continued to apply the steps God gave me to change myself no matter how long it took. The fearful thoughts, feelings, and emotions ended, and I have peace and a sound mind.

When you feel that the steps are not working, be aware that the Enemy is trying to discourage you from taking them; he wants to keep you chained to fear. Because you are aware of his plans, you will do the opposite of what your negative thoughts tell you. Get ready to open your mind, body, and soul to a spiritual transformation, the guarantee of freedom.

1st Step: Realize You Can't Do It without Christ

The hardest thing in the world can be to allow someone to take control of your life, to allow someone to invade your personal space, to put your life in his or her hands, hoping he or she has your best interest at heart. It may be a doctor you're trusting to handle your stage-4 cancer or a psychiatrist you're relying on to lead you out the mud of depression to firmer psychological ground. You may have given your life over to antidepressants, drugs, or alcohol to shake your past away. Whatever it is, you're trying to find something or someone to pull you out of that whirlpool of fear and anxiety that has you dreading the future. You look to temporary fixes to pacify your heart, mind, and soul, praying that you will find the antidote for your internal demons.

Such temporary things are never reliable; they will not ultimately deliver you from your crises. And what will you do when you can't get those drugs or see that psychiatrist? What will you do when you lose your job? In our society, we rely on material things that are not guaranteed to be there tomorrow. As others have been, I have been guilty of looking to everything else to fix my problems, for example, those magnesium pills to subdue my anxiety. It's so easy to seek quick fixes to temporarily pacify a situation, but in reality, those pills were mentally handicapping me.

I became determined not to allow a pill to dictate my happiness let alone my life. I had to get back to the basics and trust in someone I couldn't see but could feel with my heart. Through him, I was delivered. God is someone you can rely on to be by your side 24/7, 365 days a year. It's only through God that you can experience true deliverance from what you're going through that will guarantee you peace, love, joy, happiness, protection, and healing. John 16:33 kjv tells us, "These things I have spoken to you, that in me you may have peace. In the world you will have tribulation; but be of good cheer, I have overcome the world."

Christ went through ridicule, beatings, and death on the cross for our sins. He was resurrected from the dead so we could have everlasting life. God reassures us that we will be able to overcome because he has already overcome it for us. Who else is a better candidate to turn over our will to? Jesus is the one who has conquered death. Nothing can hold you down but you. Accepting Christ as your personal Savior and having faith in him will give you a peace that will carry you over all obstacles.

2nd Step: Realize Who You Are and the Power You Possess

The Enemy knows how to attack your sense of self-worth and make you feel you're unworthy, weak, and unable to overcome obstacles in your life. But when you give God your life, you will receive the gift of the Holy Spirit—the power to fight the Enemy. You will put the Enemy on notice that you will no longer be his puppet. You will take a stand because you will realize who you are, what you possess, and who you have in your life, God.

I found my inner power through studying the Word of God. I read Scriptures about the power God gave those who served him. Luke 9 shows how God gave his disciples authority over demons and diseases, and Luke 10 tells of how the seventy disciples rejoiced because the demons were subject to them in Jesus' name.

I found other passages in the Bible that built my faith in God and led me to believe that if God could do that in biblical days, he could do it for me today. In Romans 8:37, we read, "Yet in all things we are more than conquers through him who loved us." We are more than conquerors; we know we are not defeated. We know we will be victorious no matter the circumstances. We know that no matter what we go through or how we feel, no matter what's going on around us or happening to us, no matter what has been taken from us, we will stand firm in obedience to God's Word.

As long as we don't doubt God, we will remain conquerors who will demolish every trap the Enemy tries to ensnare us with. In 1 John 4:4, we read, "Ye are of God, little children, and have overcome them: because greater is he that is in you, than he that is in the world." We possess the living God who illuminates himself on the inside of us. Because we have God no devil in hell can destroy us unless you let him. We stand assured that with God, we will always be victorious, successful, determined, bold, fearless, and extraordinary in the eyes of God! We are his special treasures! Take it by force, because you're entitled to it!

3rd Step: Realize What You're Dealing With Is a Demonic Spirit

The Enemy doesn't care if you're black, white, Asian, or Indian. He doesn't care if you're upper, middle, or lower class. The Enemy will try to destroy you in any way possible. The Enemy will try to put you in the grave because he knows there's no repentance in the grave. All of your dreams, talents, should haves, and could haves will not mean a thing on the other side of the grave.

The Enemy hates the fact that you were made in the likeness of God. Yes, that's right—whether you are a Christian or a sinner, you were made in the likeness of God. The Enemy has a personal vendetta against you; he will try to sabotage your life any way possible and make you unhappy, unsuccessful, and unaccomplished. The Enemy will toss things at you to knock you off your feet to get you to stagnate in life.

The Enemy will try to get you to do things that will hurt you in the long run. The Enemy will try to get you to dwell on your fears and use them against you. You may say, "I'm not afraid of anything." You can fool yourself, but you can't fool the Enemy. He knows all your weaknesses and how to get your attention. That's why it's so important for you to be a child of God who knows what he or she is up against—a demonic spirit sent by the

Devil to oppress and possess and get Christians to doubt God. He wants you to keep you from being successful; he wants you to be weak and die.

If you don't have God on your side to help you overcome that evil spirit, it will subdue you. Having a tormented spirit of fear can lead you into the hands of other spirits that can cause depression, sickness, paranormal feelings, and anxiety, and if you're not careful, suicide.

The Devil does this so he can get you to not trust God or doubt your decision to serve God or make you angry with God so you don't give your life to God. In 2 Timothy 1:7, we read, "For God did not give you the spirit of fear but of power, love, and a sound mind." God wants to remind you that when you come against that evil spirit, you don't have to give in to it because what God put in you will override that spirit of fear. In fact, it will override every spirit that tries to destroy your life mentally, spiritually, or physically.

God gave us the power of the Holy Spirit, love that casts out all fears, and self-control that helps us not to give into those evil things but to focus on the truth of God's Word.

4th Step: Transform Your Thoughts and Put Your Weapons to Work

Realizing that you're dealing with a spirit is half the fight. The battle really takes place in your mind. If you're not careful and don't have your shield of godly thoughts up at all times, you will have antagonizing thoughts thrown at you from every angle. The Enemy will paralyze you mentally and cause you to physically lose touch with reality; your body will be under stress that could lead to ailments.

You may have thoughts that you're going to fail or die, that you'll always be a druggie or will be just like your dad or mom, a good-for-nothing. You may think God isn't real, and you may have suicidal thoughts because you feel all alone and unloved by everyone.

Countless negative thoughts can weigh on your mind and torment you, but realizing you can transform such thoughts into positive thoughts is a major step toward overcoming fear and is vital to your everyday living. In 2 Corinthians 10:4–6 kjv, we read,

> For the weapons of our warfare are not carnal, but mighty through God to the pulling down of strong holds; Casting down imaginations, and every high thing

that exalteth itself against the knowledge
of God, and bringing into captivity every
thought to the obedience of Christ;
And having in a readiness to revenge all
disobedience, when your obedience is
fulfilled.

This could be the hardest step, especially if you're used to feeling mentally defeated because you have made a habit of giving into those tormenting thoughts that say you will never be worth it or accomplish anything. Realize that no matter how hard it is, as long as you have your mind made up to not be bullied by the Enemy, God will take you off your mental roller-coaster. As you go on, you will find it becomes easier and easier. You're supposed to fill your mind with positive things that reflect God even if that means learning Scriptures that fit your situation. Learn them so you can quote them daily and be affirmed in them. That's what I had to do, and that's why I'm free today.

You don't fight the Enemy with a physical weapon but with a spiritual weapon, the Word of God. For instance, every time you think you're not going to make it, say to yourself Philippians 4:13: "I can do all things through Christ that strengthens me." If you have thoughts that someone is out to kill you, say to yourself Isaiah 54:17:

"No weapon formed against me shall prosper." If you feel all alone, say "I'm never alone because God will never leave me nor forsake me." You may think you or a loved one will never be healed, but you can say, "By his stripes I am healed (or he or she is healed)."

Fill your thoughts with pure, holy, just, lovely, and positive thoughts. You may say those Scriptures but the thoughts are still in your mind, but don't stop. Continue to believe God's Word and quote the Scriptures, because soon you will receive a peaceful mind.

And don't stop there; Romans 10:17 tells us, "So faith comes by hearing, and hearing by the word of God," and Hebrews 10:25 says, "Nor forsaking the assembling of ourselves together, as the manner of some is; but exhorting one another: and so much the more, as you see the day approaching."

A part of your weapon is belonging to a church that is a deliverance ministry; make sure that the power of God is in your church and that you receive the truth of the Word of God because you'll need it to gain spiritual strength. If you don't have a church like that or you don't go to church, trust me—all you have to do is ask God and believe he will direct you.

Another weapon of yours is your prayer life. Set aside time to pray to God. Reading and studying your Bible is essential because you will gain the truth from God's Word and learn who you are, your purpose, and who God is. The Enemy will never be able to stop the God in you from accomplishing anything positive you put your mind to.

5th Step: Be Steadfast in the Faith

Now that you know you need God and that you're dealing with a spirit, you will gain knowledge of who you are and what you possess and can start transforming your thoughts while putting your weapons to work.

You have to take the last and most vital step— being steadfast in the faith. To be steadfast is to have firm determination, to be unshakable, to endure, and to persevere no matter the odds. Being steadfast means that even though it doesn't seem that any change has taken place, you still will not allow that to cripple your hope for change and faith in God.

People give up during this step usually because they refuse to keep trusting in God because things aren't going the way they want them to. That won't be you because you're a fighter who is fully equipped to face the challenge and keep your sanity and faith in God, always expecting the best to take place.

You will acknowledge that your deliverance can take place at any moment, and you will refuse to let doubt set in because you know it can stop your change from taking place. In 1 Corinthians 15:58 kjv, we read, "Therefore, my beloved brethren, be ye steadfast, unmovable, always abounding in the work of the Lord, forasmuch as ye know that your labor is not in vain in The Lord."

Your work in the Lord is to attend church, fast, pray, read God's Word, and apply it to your life. You will allow God's love to consume your life, you will witness about God, and you will treat your neighbor as you want to be treated. Know that your hard work will not be in vain. God is saying he sees you and he's right there, carrying you through.

16

This Is Not the End

Even when a fight looks as though it is over, even if it seems you have demolished your opponent, never turn your back or drop your guard because you never know when your opponent might rise and strike you.

Now that you see, feel, and realize the deliverance from fear that has taken place in your life, know that you can't stop there; you have to keep your guard up by realizing you can't do it without Christ. Depend on God to be your source of peace, love, joy, and success; look to nothing or anyone else to take his place. Remind yourself of who you are and of the confidence you possess as a soldier for God. You have the power he gave you to defeat every Enemy that comes your way.

Realize what you're dealing with is a demonic spirit. When you use the tactics of these five lessons, you will be five steps ahead of the Devil.

Continue to transform your thoughts, and put your weapons to work by thinking on those things that are pure, holy, and of a good report. Study your Bible, pray, fast, go to church, and surround yourself with positive people. The Enemy doesn't know your future, but he knows your past and will try to bring that up every minute to intimidate you. Be steadfast and be convinced that you are free and are determined to stay free. God has equipped you already with everything you need to win the battle.